G000127963

Table of Contents

Chapter 1: Leo Personality Profile

Leo Traits: Friendly, warm-hearted, self-indulgent, generous, moody, courageous, optimistic, patriotic, sensitive, vain, altruistic, creative, confident, strong, bossy, attention-seeking, passionate, protective

Confident and Extroverted

The confident, sunny Leo nature often ensures popularity. Leos are very sociable and love to host and attend parties. They also love to talk, and some have a tendency to brag or be pompous. Negative Leo types can be bullies or snobs who have a tendency to dominate any conversation in which they participate. Fortunately, the Leo confidence (or overconfidence) more often manifests as charisma and a propensity for risk-taking than overbearing behavior.

The popularity of Leos is enhanced by their tendency to freely share time, energy, money, and affection with others. All Leos require in return is to receive a larger share of affection and adoration than the average person.

Leos are good at promoting themselves and marketing their considerable talents. They are assertive enough to get what they want out of life, and most are sufficiently capable to achieve much of what they set their minds to. Although they can be lazy around the house, Leos are hardworking and driven when something interests them.

Passionate, Protective, and Sensitive

Leos are sensual and passionate in their romantic relationships, and ferociously protective of lovers, friends, and family. Most are willing to die for what they believe in because their fervor often extends to patriotism as well.

A combination of intensity and assertiveness can manifest as belligerence in negative Leo types. Some Leos are argumentative or domineering, while others pick their battles wisely. Most are good fighters, both in a verbal argument and in a physical confrontation. However, because they are highly reactive and emotionally intense, Leos often speak or act impulsively in emotionally charged situations and regret it later on.

Forthright Leos wear their hearts on their sleeves. Despite their natural optimism, Leos tend to be moody, and if they don't receive insufficient attention, they can grow depressed and sullen. Although they are typically swift to anger and equally quick to forgive, Leos may sulk for awhile in response to minor slights, particularly blows to their pride, but they tend to recover quickly.

Creative, Vain, and Attention Seeking

A combination of creativity and a need for the spotlight suits many Leos to careers that involve either performance or working with the public in some capacity. Leos love to be the center of attention, so fame is a powerful draw for this sign.

Many Leos have dramatic talents, which may lead them into the film industry or related professions, though Leo creativity can also manifest as a talent for arts and crafts. The Leonine flair for drama causes many Leos to exaggerate when telling a good story, but with their forthright natures, they don't typically lie unless their ascendants fall in more secretive or deceptive signs.

Leos may put on excess weight due to overindulgence (most Leos eat and drink too much if given the opportunity). However, typical Leos are very appearance-conscious, which acts as a counterforce to their self-indulgence, motivating them to reign things in when their looks start to suffer. Often the confident, capable Leo persona covers some degree of low self-esteem or worries about their attractiveness, so they work hard to keep themselves looking good.

High Need for Excitement

Most Leos love flashy cars and exciting people. They usually dress to be noticed, and are bold enough to make statements, verbal or otherwise. They have the guts to put themselves forward and don't mind the whole world looking at them. In fact, they prefer it.

Leos tend to be energetic and athletic, and they love a challenge, physical or otherwise. The typical Leo possesses unusually high physical strength and a propensity for risk taking. They crave a little danger, so unless their ascendants fall in more cautious and sensible signs such as Taurus, Virgo, or Capricorn, Leos may be drawn to extreme sports, and in some cases, stormy romantic affairs with highly unsuitable partners.

Entrepreneurialism and Leadership Ability

Despite their need for a romantic partner and an admiring audience, Leos are independent and entrepreneurial by nature, and often succeed in businesses of their own. Even when working for others, Leos tend to rise through the ranks to end up in positions of authority.

Because Leos have excellent natural leadership skills and good organizational abilities, people often look to them for guidance. Leos must guard against letting this go to their heads and repress their natural inclination to be bossy, both at work and at home.

Altruistic and Generous

Most Leos are generous and helpful by nature. They love to spoil friends, family, and romantic partners, buying extravagant gifts or blowing their money on good times. Leos can't resist luxuries and the good life, even if they can't afford it. They believe that they need to have the best and that everyone they like should have the best as well. Most are also excellent cooks, and they enjoy feeding others.

Leo is suited heroics due to a combination of bravery, altruism, generosity, protectiveness, and the need to be admired. Typical Leos will stop to help someone in need, and if they have money, most have a tendency toward philanthropy. They also tend to be soft-hearted, with a particular fondness for children and animals.

The Atypical Leo

The sun sign isn't the only element that influences personality. Aspects and planetary placements, particularly the moon sign and rising sign (ascendant), are also important. For example, a Leo with Aquarius rising will be less motivated to seek personal attention and fame than a typical Leo, and will probably be less traditional, sensitive, and protective and more open-minded as well. A Virgo ascendant can have a dramatic effect on the Leo personality, making a Leo less physically demonstrative and prone to risk taking and more humble, practical, and cautious with money.

There are many websites that offer free chart calculation to determine other planetary placements and aspects. Learning these other planetary placements is recommended, as it provides a more comprehensive personality profile.

See Appendix 3 for information about other astrological influences on personality.

Chapter 2: Leo Love and Friendship

Typical Leos are very helpful and generous to their friends, lovers, and family members, and also very protective. They won't tolerate others badmouthing those they care about, and they're willing to fight about it.

Leos also have a tendency to be domineering due to a natural inclination for leadership. This can lead to friction if they date strong, independent-minded individuals, though these are exactly the sort of people that Leos are drawn to. On the positive side, the need to lead can also manifest in supportive, nurturing behavior.

Traditional and Idealistic

Typical Leos are loyal and romantic. When they fall in love, they fall heavily. They have very idealistic, traditional notions about friendship and love, tending to put people on pedestals from which they inevitably fall, leaving the Leo disappointed and heartbroken.

A betrayed Leo will not easily get over the hurt. The wounds run deep. However, loving gestures have an equally profound effect. A thoughtful gift, a home-cooked meal, or any other tangible expression of appreciation can do wonders for a Leo's mood.

Passionate and Extravagant

In a romantic relationship, Leos are passionate and extravagant. They like to make big splashy gestures and money can go fast, but it will be spent on fun activities, good food, and presents.

Leos are equally generous with their friends, paying for or cooking lavish dinners or buying rounds of drinks. They are also quick to offer assistance to those in need (with this tendency to burn through money, Leos can develop serious financial problems).

Affectionate and Attention-Seeking

Leos need a lot of attention, perhaps even admiration, but they are willing to give the same to their partners and friends. They are very physically affectionate, and do best with friends and lovers who are also physically demonstrative.

While they prefer to be the center of attention, Leos are as generous with affectionate gestures as they are with money and time. The typical Leo is selfish only in the emotional realm. When Leos have unmet emotional needs, they are not sensitive to the emotional needs of others until their own requirements have been fulfilled.

Sensitive and Moody

Leos are quite sensitive and moody, and this tendency, combined with their need to be admired, means that they don't take criticism from partners or friends very well. Typical Leos are affectionate and loving toward their mates, except when they feel they have been slighted, at which point they can cool significantly for a while.

On the positive side, when Leos do forgive, they usually forgive completely. Like all the fire signs, they are swift to anger but get over things quickly as well.

Active, Extroverted, and Optimistic

The typical Leo is physically active and extroverted, and enjoys a bit of risk-taking. Most Leos prefer to get out, do things, and meet people rather than sitting around the house.

Leos tend to be cheerful, good-natured, confident, and optimistic, which can be uplifting for those around them. They do best with energetic, playful companions who provide the attention they need and aren't inclined to take advantage of their generous, trusting natures.

Chapter 3: Leo Compatibility with Other Sun Signs

Note: There is more to astrological compatibility than sun signs alone. Other elements in a person's natal zodiac also play a role. Ascendants (rising signs), moon signs, and other planetary placements and aspects also shape personality and affect compatibility. For example, a Capricorn with Leo rising will be more extroverted than a typical Capricorn, and a Taurus with Aries rising or the moon in Sagittarius will be more compatible with Sagittarius than a typical Taurus. For more information on other natal chart elements, see Appendix 3.

Leo + Aries

This is a passionate combination, and also very high on the compatibility scale. Both signs tend to be affectionate, bold, extroverted, and inclined to seek excitement and novelty, so these two can have a blast together. However, both will want to be the center of attention, which could lead to friction and drama (and fights will be as passionate as romance with this pair).

Although both signs tend to have similar social drives, Leo is more concerned with appearances, so Aries impulsivity in social situations can lead to agonizing social embarrassment for Leo. In addition, there will probably be struggles for dominance with this pair. Both Aries and Leo will want to be the boss, and neither can tolerate being ordered about, so they may end up deadlocked over a variety of issues. An excess of pride and ego on both sides can cause the downfall of this relationship.

On the plus side, this is an exciting combination, both for friendship and romance. And because both individuals tend to be generous and warm-hearted, it has the potential to be a mutually supportive and loving match. However, its success is will hinge upon the ability of both individuals to compromise and allow one another to take the lead in certain situations, and neither sign finds this easy.

Aries and Leo tend to be compatible in terms of lifestyle preferences. They share a need to stay active and a strong competitive streak that can lend excitement and challenge to the relationship. These two will want to get out and socialize on a regular basis, and they're likely to cultivate a wide circle of friends together (unless their ascendants fall in shyer signs). Both Aries and Leo also tend to be creative, athletic, or both, which provides plenty of common ground for the development of shared interests.

Leo + Taurus

This is a passionate combination, but also challenging. Taurus and Leo can irritate each other because their personalities are so different. Typical Leos are boisterous, attention-seeking risk takers, while Tauruses tend to be mellow, laid back, pragmatic individuals (unless they have their ascendants in fire signs). To make matters worse, these two signs share the trait of stubbornness, so if they hit a point of conflict, neither is likely to give an inch. As a result, they can end up with a stalemate that poisons the relationship.

On the plus side, Taurus will appreciate Leo's affectionate nature and Leo will respond well to Taurean sensuality in a romantic relationship. Interestingly, this combination may work better in romance than in friendship, at least in the short term. However, different lifestyle preferences can be a problem in the long run if these two move in together.

Taurus and Leo tend to have very different ideas about what constitutes a good life. Although both love luxury, decadence, and good food, Tauruses tend to be sensible spenders, whereas Leos are spendthrifts who show no restraint when it comes to buying a good time. This means that Taurus may become distressed at the prospect of Leo bankrupting the couple, while Leo may find Taurus's financial caution oppressive. The typical Leo also has a stronger drive to get out and meet people at a variety of venues, while the typical Taurus is happy to spend time with a few close friends in someone's home.

Another problem with this pairing is that Leo craves attention and admiration, and if there is not enough of this forthcoming at home, will seek it externally, triggering feelings of jealousy in Taurus. Leo may also fail to appreciate the finer Taurean qualities such as stability, dedication, and tolerance. While others admire these traits, they are likely to bore Leo, who is more impressed by glamor and risk taking. Taurus, in turn, is unlikely to appreciate some of Leo's more dynamic qualities, perceiving assertiveness and a talent for self-promotion as egotism and arrogance. However, Taurus will admire Leo's courage and protectiveness, and Leo will appreciate Taurus's supportiveness, loyalty, and quiet strength.

Getting along day to day may be challenging for this pair unless other elements in their natal zodiacs are more favorable. However, they do share a creative spark, so they may bond over artistic pursuits, and they also share a love of good food, luxury, and other material pleasures, so there is plenty of common ground upon which to build a relationship.

In a best-case scenario, these two will compromise on points of contention and help each other overcome their respective weaknesses. If they are willing to learn from one another, Taurus can help Leo develop some much-needed financial restraint (and in some cases, physical caution as well), and Leo can encourage Taurus to take more risks and socialize with new people from time to time.

Leo + Gemini

Gemini-Leo is a fun combination. Both individuals tend to be childlike, spontaneous, and playful, unless other elements in their natal zodiacs incline them toward seriousness. Leo's optimism and confidence soothes Gemini's anxieties, while vivacious, unpredictable Gemini holds Leo's interest and prevents things from becoming dull. Both signs tend to be friendly and sociable, so they will enjoy going out and doing things together. However, although compatibility is high with this match, there may be a few points of contention.

One issue on which these two signs don't usually see eye-to-eye is the desire for novelty. Although Leos enjoy a good adventure, in day-to-day life they tend stick with the things, ideas, activities, and people they know and like, whereas Geminis crave novelty. This can create problems when Leo remains loyal to all he or she loves while Gemini wanders off in search of something untried. This can make Leo feel insecure and jealous (particularly if Gemini's outside interests include other people), and Gemini may be irritated by Leo's possessiveness and need for attention. However, in a best-case scenario, Leo will help Gemini cultivate deeper connections with people, places, and ideas, while Gemini will encourage Leo to try new things and seek new experiences.

In a romantic relationship, Leo might push Gemini for more commitment and personal attention than Gemini is ready or able to give, and suffer insecurity in response to Gemini's emotional detachment. Leo may also be irritated by Gemini's social butterfly tendencies because Leos like to be the center of attention. To make matters worse, the infamous Leo pride may be wounded by Gemini's tendency to poke fun at others. However, despite these issues, Gemini and Leo should get along quite well in day-to-day life (unless other elements in their natal zodiacs are unfavorable) because their lifestyle preferences tend to be similar and they also have some complementary abilities that are beneficial to their relationship. Leos, with their strong organizational skills and perseverance, are better at seeing things through and dealing with the responsibilities of day-to-day life, while Geminis have a talent for keeping things fresh and interesting so that Leos don't grow bored.

This pair does suffer from a significant flaw that can create problems in business and romantic relationships: both tend to be bad with money. The typical Leo is a decadent spendthrift, and Gemini tends to be impulsive, acting in the moment with little thought for the consequences. As a result, these two may spiral into bankruptcy together unless their ascendants are in more pragmatic signs such as Cancer, Capricorn, Virgo, or Taurus. Neither is inclined to have a restraining effect on the other, so this pair will need to keep a close eye on their finances.

Leo + Cancer

This match has potential. Cancers can give Leos the devotion and attention they crave and Leos provide plenty of affection in return, which Cancers find reassuring. These are both very warm-hearted and demonstrative signs, so there is a good chance of success here, though these two may clash when Cancer wants quiet evenings at home or to go on a peaceful hike or mellow pub outing and Leo wants to go out on the town. Leos crave excitement, while Cancers want security and stability, so these two can be at cross-purposes. Although both are romantic, romance to a Leo means passion and fireworks, whereas for a Cancer it is emotional fulfillment and comfort. Leo extravagance is also at odds with Cancer practicality, so conflicts over money are likely.

Another problem with the Leo Cancer pairing is the fact that both signs tend to be highly sensitive, though Leo is more likely to hide this vulnerability. Cancers can be easily hurt by offhand remarks, and Leos are easily wounded by anything that affects their self-esteem. The success of this relationship will likely depend on the ability of both individuals to treat one another gently and compromise when it comes to shared activities. Cancer will also need to flatter Leo on a regular basis, and Leo will need to provide reassurance when necessary and show compassion when Cancer suffers from insecurity or sadness. This match works best if their ascendants and moon signs bring their temperaments into closer alignment (for example, a Leo with a Cancer or Taurus ascendant or a Cancer with an Aries or Leo ascendant).

On the positive side, these two can form a nice complement to one another. Leo's sunny, optimistic disposition can act as a potent natural antidepressant for moody Cancer, and Cancer's pragmatism can keep Leo from spending all their money. Also, Cancer typically has no desire to dominate or control, so Leo's pride won't be threatened (Leos prefer to lead and Cancers appreciate strong partners). Both also tend to be good cooks, green thumbs, romantic idealists, and generous gift givers, so there is plenty to hold these two together unless other elements in their natal zodiacs are highly unfavorable.

Leo + Leo

When two Leos pair up, there tend to be plenty of fireworks. Friendships will probably be somewhat competitive, and romances will passionate in both the positive and negative senses. Each member of this pair will want to be the leader and the center of attention, so these two strong personalities will probably either clash early on or warm to each other right from the start. A Leo-Leo connection tends to be beautiful or ugly, with no middle ground.

A double dose of Leo can be a lot of fun in love or friendship, and there is the potential to forge a strong connection. Two Leos are likely to have shared interests and lifestyle preferences, as well as a mutual need for excitement keeps things from getting dull. On the negative side, both individuals are proud, stubborn, competitive, and somewhat self-absorbed. Although warm and generous with their time, money, and affection, Leos can be emotionally selfish because they need a lot of adoration. They do best with devoted partners who lavish affection on them, so both members of a Leo-Leo pair may feel that they're being shortchanged in terms of attention and emotional support. There is also no one to rein in the spending with this extravagant pair, so there is a risk that these two will end up with nothing unless their ascendants fall in more restrained signs.

One very positive aspect of this match is that Leos tend to be exuberant and optimistic, which can bring a sunny, positive energy to their relationships. They are also likely to have a good social life together and spoil one another with lavish gifts, fine food, and other luxuries. One or both will likely have a talent for cooking, gardening, or decorating, which can enhance their home life, and because they tend to be creative, two Leos may also bond over shared artistic pursuits or practical crafts.

In a business partnership, a pair of Leos will have plenty of great ideas and promotional talent, but may lack the practicality required to make a success of their venture unless other elements in their natal zodiacs incline them toward greater pragmatism. Leos are good at generating winning ideas, getting things started, promoting, and organizing at a high level, but they typically lack the patience required to complete the less glamorous detail work.

Leo + Virgo

This match can be challenging because these two signs have such different ways of relating to the world. Leo may find Virgo too private and cautious, and Virgo will probably find Leo too desperate for praise and attention. Virgo is intellectually focused and somewhat aloof, which can be upsetting for passionate, affectionate Leo. Leo, in turn, tends to be noisy, boisterous, and prone to risk taking, which can be stressful for quiet, careful Virgo.

One of the most significant difficulties with this pairing is that Leo is proud and sensitive to criticism, while Virgo is contemptuous of large egos and compelled to deflate them. Leos may suffer devastating blows to their self-esteem when Virgos make unflattering judgments (what Virgo considers constructive criticism is likely to be perceived as a personal attack by Leo). Leos are also likely to find emotionally reserved Virgos insufficiently demonstrative and romantic. To make matters worse, the typical Leo is also more sociable than the typical Virgo, and is unlikely to understand Virgo's greater need for time alone (Leo may even take this as a personal rejection). In a romantic relationship, Virgo will probably find Leo's need for attention and adoration perplexing and irritating, and Leo will may find Virgo asocial and dull.

The primary reason why Virgos need solitary time or prefer to spend time with small groups of friends is that they are prone to anxiety and thrive in calm environments. Typical Leos, by contrast, are energized by noisy, action-packed environments, so these two may disagree about social activities.

Another problem with this pairing is that Leos tend to be emotionally expressive and quick to anger (though also quick to forgive), while Virgos are inclined to avoid conflict (and those who provoke it). This clash of styles can leave Virgo in a chronic state of distress, and Virgo is quick to leave (or at least retreat from) strife-ridden situations.

An additional difference between these two is that Leos tend to show their love with grand romantic words and gestures, whereas Virgos typically do so through considerate practical actions and useful gifts. In a positive relationship, this could be beneficial, as both will enjoy doing things for each other. However, in a negative relationship, Leo may find Virgo's gifts boring and unromantic, while Virgo finds Leo's presents unnecessarily expensive and useless (a typical Leo is more likely to appreciate gifts of fine food, expensive alcoholic beverages, or luxury items, while a typical Virgo would rather give or receive a practical gift).

The success of this relationship will probably depend Virgo's willingness to be more careful with Leo's delicate pride and more overtly affectionate, and Leo's ability to rein in the spending and grow a thicker skin when it comes to taking criticism. In a best-case scenario, Leo will help Virgo lighten up and become less anxious and more sociable, and Virgo will help Leo develop the self-restraint and diligence necessary to do something productive with Leo's many creative and potentially lucrative ideas.

Virgo and Leo often share some common ground in the form of interests and activities that may increase the likelihood of relationship success. Leos tend to be creative and typical Virgos enjoy practical crafts or building things, so these two may engage in creative, constructive pursuits together. Virgos also like home-based activities such as gardening and cooking nutritious food, and Leos tend to have green thumbs and a flare for cooking and baking as well (though they are more inclined to focus on decadent treats than health-promoting meals). Both signs like to be active, so they may also share an interest in sports or rugged outdoor hobbies. In addition, health-conscious Virgos tend to stay in relatively good shape, which is important to appearance-conscious Leos. If these two have shared interests and other elements in their natal zodiacs are more compatible, this match has potential.

Leo + Libra

This is a great combination, both for friendship and romance. These two tend to get along well because Libra appreciates

Leo's decisiveness and strength of character, and Leo loves Libra's wit, charm, and style. However, Leo might find Libra a bit too easy going or even weak (Leos respect Leonine traits such as forcefulness and dominance, even though they find them difficult to live with in another person). This lack of respect for Libran mellowness could reduce the potency of a romantic relationship, but for the most part, these two are well-matched and often share common interests and lifestyle preferences.

Both signs have a decadent streak, so they may bond over the pursuit of luxury. These two friendly, extroverted individuals can also have a great social life together because both love to get out, meet people, and be admired. In addition, they share a strong romantic streak, which is beneficial for serious relationships. On the other hand, both tend to fall in love with idealized versions of their partners rather than their real selves, which can lead to disappointment. To make matters worse, they also tend to fall in love with the idea of being love, but may have difficulty with the duller or more difficult day-to-day aspects of living with others once the initial bloom of passion has faded.

Although both Leo and Libra like a lot of attention, Libras are usually happy to let Leos be the leaders and the centers of attention (or at least let them think that they are), which helps to prevent conflicts. Libras are tolerant and egalitarian by nature, so they don't try to dominate their partners. This means that Libra is less likely to threaten Leo's sense of power and control. Libra is also not inclined to pick fights, which can keep things harmonious. However, some Leos may see their Libra partners' efforts to keep things calm and smooth as a lack of passion. On the other hand, Libran tact and diplomacy reduce the risk that Leo's ego will be punctured by a careless word or sharp criticism.

There are some differences in the ways that Leo and Libra perceive the world, which can cause misunderstandings. Leos run on emotion, while Libras process things intellectually. Loyal, emotional Leos passionately defend those they care about, while detached, reasonable Libras can see both sides of an issue and tend to make their judgments based on fairness rather than favoritism. This may lead to problems if Leo demands that Libra take a side in a conflict but Libra stubbornly maintains a rational, neutral stance. If Leo perceives Libra as disloyal, this can be a deal breaker. However, if these two can meet each other halfway, with Leo making an effort to understand other perspectives and Libra showing absolute loyalty in particularly sensitive situations, their differing views of conflict are unlikely to create serious problems.

Leo + Scorpio

This is a passionate but challenging combination. These two are often drawn together, but getting along in day-to-day life will be difficult unless other elements in their natal zodiacs are more compatible. In a worst-case scenario, this combustible match will lead to an endless clash of wills or a series of exhausting power struggles.

Scorpio and Leo typically have little in common other than intensity and a propensity for risk taking. Scorpios tend to be secretive and somewhat introverted, while Leos are socially oriented and wear their hearts on their sleeves. When these two pair up, Leo may find Scorpio temperamental and demanding, while Scorpio finds Leo egotistical and self-absorbed. To make matters worse, their shared traits of stubbornness, pride, and inflexibility are more likely to trigger conflict than encourage bonding. Also, Leo's need to go out, socialize with others on a regular basis (and even flirt a bit) is likely to trigger Scorpio's jealousy, and perceptive Scorpio will know exactly how to strike the most devastating retaliatory blows to Leo's delicate pride.

In a romantic relationship, this combination is exciting in the bedroom but prone to conflict everywhere else. It can be difficult for two such strong-willed individuals to live together unless other elements in their natal zodiacs incline them to be more compromising or at least bring their temperaments into better alignment.

Despite its many difficulties, there are some positive elements to this match. Both signs are inclined to be loyal when they find someone they really like, and emotional friction keeps things from getting boring. Both individuals also tend to be thrill-seekers and they are good at keeping their cool in dangerous situations, so they may bond over a shared love of extreme sports, other dangerous pastimes, or risky business endeavors. If these two can develop greater flexibility in their day-to-day interactions and learn to let things go, they can reduce the likelihood that their relationship will be torn apart by conflict.

Leo + Sagittarius

This is a fun, optimistic, cheerful combination. Both signs are naturally exuberant, extroverted, and adventurous, so there is bound to be plenty of excitement when these two get together.

Leo and Sagittarius both tend to be active, so they may bond over a love of sports or other energetic pursuits. However, they also share a proclivity for self-indulgence, and must guard against the tendency to eat and drink too much and blow all their money on good times and impractical or unrealistic plans. These two could end up in poor health, bankrupt, or mired in other troubles due to a mutual lack of restraint (this pairing may not be ideal for business partnerships unless at least one of the individuals has a more pragmatic ascendant).

The day-to-day compatibility of these two signs is quite high, which is great for friendship as well as romance, and they also have some complementary traits that are beneficial in a romantic relationship. Sagittarius can introduce Leo to new ideas and experiences, while Leo brings fiery passion to the match to hold Sagittarius's interest. Both tend to prefer getting out and doing things rather than spending cozy evenings at home, so they are more likely than many other sun sign combinations to agree when it comes to activity choices.

One potential difficulty with this pairing is that Leos tend to be romantic and somewhat possessive, whereas the typical Sagittarius is not so commitment-oriented (though a Sagittarius with a more stable rising sign such as Taurus is more likely to stick around). Even when Sagittarians do make monogamous commitments, they tend to be irritated by any sign of neediness or jealousy in a partner. Leo, on the other hand, craves personal attention and public demonstrations of loyalty, and may feel insecure with an independent Sagittarius.

Another problem with this pairing is that Sagittarius tends to be insensitive and overly blunt, and Leo pride is easily wounded. There is a risk that a few ill-chosen words will drive a wedge between these two. However, although both are feisty individuals and quick to anger, they also tend to be forgiving, so it may be possible to smooth things over, given the strong general compatibility between these two signs.

Leo + Capricorn

This is not a great combination unless other elements in their natal zodiacs are more compatible. Capricorn's emotional reserve is disturbing to Leo, who likes forthright expressiveness and lots of attention. Leo tends to be quite affectionate and wants plenty of romance, physical demonstrativeness, and praise in return. Capricorn tends to be more reticent, disliking public displays of affection and taking some time to warm up to new people. The typical Capricorn is also ambitious and busy, and may lack the time to provide the personal attention that Leo requires (or not even understand the need to do so). Humble Capricorn is also inclined to see Leo's need for compliments as a sign of egotism.

Another significant problem with this match is that Leo is likely to find Capricorn overly cautious with money, while Capricorn will be distressed or angered by Leo's extravagance. Leos like to live large and they don't deny themselves or their partners anything, even if it means going into debt. Capricorns, by contrast, tend to scrimp and save because they require financial security to feel safe. These different financial styles could potentially lead to fights over money in a romantic relationship or a business partnership.

Further complications arise when Leo wants to dominate and make all the decisions, because Capricorn fears losing control. Capricorns have a strong need to be in charge of their fates, and the typical Capricorn is not happy to sit back and let others take the lead, but Leo is a natural leader and wants to be in the driver's seat at all times. Both are strong-willed signs, which can lead to clashes.

Capricorns also tend to be more socially restrained than Leos. Leos like to get out and mingle, and the typical Leo is more likely to enjoy team sports than solo pursuits. Capricorns also like to stay active, though the typical Capricorn is drawn to fitness activities that can be done alone or with a close friend or two, such as running, hiking, skiing, or cycling. And when Capricorns spend time socializing, they usually prefer smaller gatherings to large, raucous parties, and they seek the company of trusted long-term companions over that of unknown individuals and acquaintances. Leos, by contrast, want to get out and meet new people on a regular basis.

Overall, these two signs have vastly different approaches to life. In a worst-case scenario, Leo will be a constant irritant to Capricorn and Capricorn will act as a wet blanket for Leo. On the other hand, both signs tend to be loyal and commitment-oriented unless other elements in their natal zodiacs incline them toward uncharacteristic casualness. Also, both like to be active, so they may introduce one another to new physical activities. In a best-case scenario, these two will have positive effects on one another, with Leo's warmth melting Capricorn's cool exterior and Capricorn helping Leo develop some much-needed self-control and financial sense.

Leo + Aquarius

This can be a difficult combination. Aquarians are more cerebral than physical, while Leos are very emotionally expressive and physically demonstrative. Leos need frequent assurances of love and attraction that Aquarians are often lax in giving. As a result, Leo may end up feeling unloved in this pairing, while Aquarius finds Leo overly needy.

These two also tend to differ politically and in terms of preferred lifestyles, with Leos typically being more conventional and Aquarians gravitating toward unusual political views and lifestyle choices. To make matters worse, Leos want the lion's share of their partners' attention, while Aquarians tend to divide their time equally among all those in their lives. Loyal Leos need special treatment to feel secure in a relationship, but fair-minded Aquarians tend to treat everyone they like similarly, which can create problems in a romantic relationship.

Another point of contention between these two signs is that Leos are appearance-conscious, while typical Aquarians have little interest in surface things. Aquarians are concerned with ideas and philosophies, so Leo's interest in clothing, social status, and glamorous events and people will seem shallow to Aquarius, while many Aquarian pursuits (and friends) will seem eccentric or even crazy to Leo.

Aquarius wants lots of personal freedom and will probably find Leo too possessive and demanding, and Leo may find Aquarius cold and aloof. However, if other elements in their natal zodiacs are more compatible, this can be interesting and intellectually stimulating match, and these two individuals may have positive effects on one another. Leos can benefit from cultivating some Aquarian detachment to reduce their sensitivity to criticism, and they will expand their horizons by adopting a more open-minded Aquarian approach to life. Leos, in turn, can act as stabilizing forces for Aquarians, who are so open to new ideas that they may ruin their lives in the service of crackpot theories and ideologies (or even dangerous people in extreme cases).

Leo + Pisces

This can be a very intense and passionate combination in a romantic relationship, though these two are not particularly compatible. Leos tend to be extroverted and excitement seeking, whereas Pisceans become over-stimulated in noisy, chaotic environments. Typical Leos are relentlessly sociable, while Pisceans need plenty of time on their own to recharge their batteries, and they are likely to find the Leonine social whirlwind draining. Leo may perceive the Piscean need spend time alone as a rejection, and Pisces may find Leo overwhelming. Each will probably seem overly needy to the other, though in different ways. Leo will have trouble coping with Pisces's dark moods, and Pisces will probably find Leo too demanding (Leos want plenty of attention and can't stand to be ignored).

Despite its shortcomings, there are also some positive aspects to this pairing. The typical Pisces has no need to dominate or control others, happily letting Leo take the lead on many issues. Both signs tend to be romantic, affectionate, and idealistic, though they may also be unrealistic, putting one another up on pedestals from which they inevitably fall. Pisces will appreciate Leo's protectiveness and be impressed by Leo's self-confidence, while Leo will be intrigued by the fascinating Piscean personality. Both individuals tend to be altruistic rescuers, so they may bond over the common ground of helping other people, animals, or environmental causes. Both also tend to be creative, which provides opportunities to enjoy shared activities. However, getting along day-to-day can be difficult for this pair.

With Leo and Pisces, there tends to be a clash of preferred lifestyles. Leo wants to get out more, seeking the excitement of a crowd (and an admiring audience), whereas Pisces prefers to stick close to home or go out for some quieter activity such as a hike or dinner at a restaurant. In a romantic relationship, Pisces tends to be more open-minded and adventurous in the bedroom, whereas Leo, though passionate, is usually more conventional.

There is also a disconnect in the ways in which these two signs relate to the world. Pisces is deep, changeable, and complex, and has a tendency to withdraw when under stress to regroup and contemplate options, whereas Leo is direct, straightforward, and uncomplicated, preferring to tackle things head on and swiftly. These two may have trouble relating to one another unless other elements in their natal zodiacs bring their temperaments into closer alignment. To make matters worse, they share a penchant for self-indulgence, which means that they may bond over unhealthful pursuits such as excessive eating and or substance abuse.

Chapter 4: Leo Marriage

Traditional astrological wisdom holds that Leos are most compatible with Aries, Gemini, Libra, and Sagittarius, and least compatible Taurus, Virgo, Scorpio, Capricorn, Aquarius, and Pisces. But what do the actual marriage and divorce statistics say?

Mathematician Gunter Sachs (1998) conducted a large-scale study of sun signs, encompassing nearly one million people in Switzerland, which found statistically significant results on a number of measures including marriage and divorce. Castille (2000) conducted a similar study in France using marriage statistics collected between 1976 and 1997, which included more than six million marriages. Findings from these studies are summarized below.

Leo Men

The Sachs Study

Leo men marry Aries women most often in Switzerland, while they are least likely to marry Aquarians. They are also least likely to divorce Aries women. However, contrary to conventional astrological wisdom, Leo men are more likely to divorce Libra women than those of any other sign. The following is an overall ranking from most common to least common marriages with Leo men (* indicates that the result is statistically significant—in other words, the effect is very large):

1. Aries*

2. Cancer

3. Capricorn

4. Pisces

5. Virgo

6. Leo

7. Scorpio

8. Libra

9. Taurus

10. Gemini

11. Sagittarius

12. Aquarius*

Marriage rates for various signs are similar, with the exceptions of Aries and Aquarius.

Leo men and Aries women may do well together because both tend to be extroverted, excitement-seeking, risk-taking, and energetic, so they are likely to enjoy doing many of the same things. Both tend to have a creative streak as well.

As for the bottom of the list, Aquarius is Leo's opposite sign, and the two tend to be pulled in very different directions. Typical Leos are physical, down-to-earth, warm, affectionate, expressive, and passionate, whereas typical Aquarians are emotionally detached, tending to experience the world via thoughts more than feelings, so they are usually calm and independent by nature. Because of these differing ways of perceiving and interacting with the world, a Leo may find the typical Aquarian cold and distant, whereas the Aquarian may find that the Leo requires too much individual attention (Aquarians usually prefer to spend their social time with groups or various individuals rather than a single person). However, if the ascendants or moon signs are more compatible, these two can make an interesting match.

What accounts for the higher-than-average divorce statistic between the theoretically compatible signs of Leo and Libra? Typical Libras can be quite flirtatious, and typical Leos want to be the center of attention, so this is one possible trigger for relationship problems. Also, Libras tend to be calm and rational, able to see both sides of an issue, whereas Leos often gravitate firmly toward one side in any argument and defend it with a fierce intensity. Differences in the way the two signs deal with contentious issues could lead to clashes.

The Castille Study

Castille found that Leo men in France were most likely to marry Leo women, and least likely to marry Scorpios. The following is an overall ranking from most common to least common marriages with Leo men (* indicates that the result is statistically significant):

1. Leo*

2. Libra

3. Virgo

4. Pisces

5. Gemini

6. Aquarius

7. Cancer

8. Aries

9. Capricorn

10. Sagittarius

11. Taurus

12. Scorpio*

The top choices for Leo men are unsurprising. Two Leos are bound to have some common ground, and Libra is thought to be one of Leo's more compatible signs (though the Sachs study suggests that this doesn't always last). An astrologer wouldn't necessarily expect to find Virgo among the top three as the Virgo caution and modesty are at odds with Leo risk-taking and attention-seeking, but Virgos often have personal planets such as Mercury, Venus, and Mars in Leo (personal planets stay close to the sun), which may raise the compatibility level.

Finding Sagittarius, Scorpio, and Taurus at the bottom of the list is also unsurprising. Although Sagittarius and Leo should be compatible for friendship, the typical Sagittarius may not give a Leo the personal attention he needs (Sagittarians tend to be quite independent and are apt to take off in search of new adventures if things grow too settled). As for Taurus, this sign is often too pragmatic and laid back for Leo, and the Leo tendency to burn through money with nothing to show for it will drive the typical Taurus crazy.

With Scorpio, there tends to be a clash of wills, as each side fights for power and control within the relationship. Of course, if the two individuals have very compatible rising signs or moon signs, opposing tendencies are likely to be minimized.

Leo Women

Sachs Study

With regard to who Leo women are most inclined to marry in Switzerland, Sachs found no statistically significant result for any sign. However, he did find that they are least likely to marry Taurus men, which is in keeping with traditional astrological theory. Leo women probably bypass Taurus men more often than those of any other sign because they may find the typical Taurus too predictable and habit-bound (though a Taurus whose ascendant is in a fire sign should be far more dynamic). The following is an overall ranking from most common to least common marriages with Leo women (* indicates that the result is statistically significant—in other words, the effect is very large):

1. Libra

2. Aries

3. Aquarius

4. Sagittarius

5. Leo

6. Cancer

7. Scorpio

8. Gemini

9. Capricorn

10. Pisces

11. Virgo

12. Taurus*

Seeing Libra at the top of the marriage list is no surprise. Libra and Leo often attract one another. Both signs tend to be drawn toward physical and cultural activities and social pursuits, so there is likely to be common ground. Furthermore, Libra has a sense of style that Leo appreciates, while Leo's assertiveness and confidence are appealing to typical Libras.

The divorce statistics for Leo women provide some surprises: Leo women are most likely to divorce the theoretically compatible signs of Aries and Sagittarius, and least likely to divorce the supposedly incompatible sign of Aquarius, as well as the sign most often divorced by Leo men—Libra.

While Leo men may be attracted to Aries competitiveness (and even combativeness in some cases), Leo women may not find it as appealing. In a culture that raises boys to be more aggressive, the natural assertiveness of Aries may be exacerbated to a point where some female Leos find it a bit overwhelming.

Sagittarian spouses may not last because they usually always have their eyes on the horizon, looking for new experiences. A Leo who does receive enough of her lover's focus will be quick to move on (as will a typical Sagittarius who feels that his freedom is being curtailed).

Why are marriages between the opposite signs of Leo and Aquarius more inclined to last? Despite a need for plenty of interpersonal freedom, Aquarians can be quite loyal when they find a person who meets their eccentric criteria. And although the emotional styles of the two signs are at odds, there is also the common ground of extroversion and generosity that may bridge the gap.

Castille Study

The Castille study found the highest rates of marriage between Leo women and Leo men in France. Castille also found that Leo women are least likely to marry Taurus and Aquarius men. The following is an overall ranking from most common to least common marriages with Leo women (* indicates that the result is statistically significant):

1. Leo*

2. Virgo

3. Sagittarius

4. Libra

5. Cancer

6. Aries

7. Pisces

8. Gemini

9. Capricorn

10. Scorpio

11. Aquarius*

12. Taurus*

The Castille study provided no surprises for Leo women's marriage statistics, save for the second-place position of Virgo. However, given that personal planets (Mercury, Venus, and Mars) stay close to the sun sign, many Virgos will have personal planets in Leo (and many Leos will have personal planets in Virgo), which probably enhances compatibility in some pairings.

Seeing Aquarius near the bottom of the list is to be expected. Sensitive, passionate, expressive Leo may have to fight to get the attention and affection she needs from an emotionally detached, independent Aquarius. Interestingly, while Leo women often bypass Aquarius men (at least in France), when they do get married, the Sachs study suggests that it has have better-than-average staying power. This may reflect the fact that when Aquarians actually manage to find a partner who meets their eccentric criteria, they are inclined to stick with the relationship.

The Best Match for Leo

The best match for Leos of either gender is apparently another Leo (and Aries for Leo men), whereas Taurus and Scorpio may be among the more difficult matches. However, Leo people who find themselves romantically entangled with one of the less compatible signs should not despair. Plenty of marriages between supposedly incompatible signs have lasted.

It's important to keep in mind that these are statistical tendencies; this doesn't mean that every romance between incompatible signs is doomed. For example, out of 6,498,320 marriages encompassing all possible sign combinations in the Castille study, there were 949 *more* marriages between Leo men and Leo women than would be expected if sun signs had no effect, whereas between Leo men and Scorpio women, there were 446 *fewer* marriages than would be expected if pairings were random. However, there still were many marriages between the supposedly least compatible signs.

Astrology is complex, and there is more to take into account than just sun signs. Two people with incompatible sun signs may have highly compatible rising signs or moon signs that can make the difference between a bad match and a good match with a bit of an "edge" that keeps things interesting.

*The Sachs study has been criticized for not taking potential confounding variables into account and continues to be controversial. I have found no critiques of the Castille study thus far.

Chapter 5: Leo Careers

Fire sign people (Aries, Leo, and Sagittarius) need excitement, variety, and opportunities to interact. They should avoid jobs that are sedentary or solitary, and repetitive detail work. The ideal career for a fire sign will offer some degree of flexibility, as Aries and Leo always want to run the show and Sagittarius has an exaggerated need for personal freedom.

Leo Career Aptitudes

Leos do best in jobs where they can be noticed and admired, and in which they can put their creative and dramatic talents to good use. With physical strength and confidence, they are also suited to athletic careers and other physically demanding occupations.

Leos have a strong aesthetic sense, which can lead some into fashion and design. This sign is also known for exceptional organizational ability and leadership skills, suiting many Leos to high managerial positions. In addition, Leos are often good cooks and green thumbs, so work with food or plants is also a possibility.

Leos should avoid careers where they will work alone. Jobs that provide the opportunity to meet and interact with lots of people are best, as Leos tend to be friendly and have good social skills, unless their ascendants fall in more introverted signs. Many Leos are also good with children and animals.

Leo careers and career fields include actor/actress, animal trainer, anything to do with the media or public relations, athlete, business manager, chairman/woman, charity organizer, clothing designer, cook/chef, dancer, director, event planner/coordinator, gardener, hairdresser, hospitality industry worker, host/hostess, interior designer/decorator, lawyer, managing director, model, painter, radio host, self-employed business person, talent agent and/or promoter, teacher, writer, and youth worker.

Appendix 1: Leo Associations

Leo Ruling Planet: Sun

Symbol: The lion

Element: Fire

Quality: Fixed

Metal: Gold

Gemstones: Amber, ruby, carnelian, peridot (August)

Associated Parts of the Body: Heart, upper back, spleen, head

Number: 1

Places Associated with Leo: Romania, Italy, France, Rome, Prague, Bath, Bristol, Los Angeles, Chicago, Damascus, Philadelphia, Hollywood

Associated Animals: Swan, lion, seal, cat, rainbow salmon

Associated Trees: Birch, holly, hazel, trees bearing citrus fruit

Associated Plants and Herbs: Rosemary, saffron, juniper, chamomile, frankincense, mistletoe, angelica, bay, marigold, sunflower

Associated Foods: Lemon, orange, hazelnut, sunflower seed, almond

Leo Colours: Gold, yellow, bright blue, royal purple

Associated Patterns or Design Motifs: Bold solid blocks of bright colour (no fussy patterns)

Other Leo Associations: Luxury items, trophies, perfume, fireplaces, parties, limousines, jewelry, sports, entertainment, ceremonies, children, art, culture, the stock market, the lottery, flashy cars, extravagance, royalty, egotism, narcissism, generosity, grandiosity, entertaining, decadence, rich foods, showing off, style, lavish spending, fame, leadership

Appendix 2: Famous Leos

Aldous Huxley, Alex Haley, Alexandre Dumas, Alfred
Hitchcock, Alfred Lord Tennyson, Amelia Earhart, Andy
Warhol, Angela Bassett, Anna Paquin, Antonia Banderas,
Arnold Swarzenegger, Barack Obama, Beatrix Potter, Ben
Affleck, Benito Mussolini, Bindi Irwin, Booth Tarkington, Cain
Velasquez, Carl Jung, Carroll O'Connor, Casey Affleck,
Casey Stengel, Cecil B. DeMille, Charles Bukowski, Charlize
Theron, Chief Dan George, Chris Hemsworth, Christian
Slater, Claude Debussy, Coco Chanel, Connie Chung,
Coolio, Daniel Radcliffe, Danielle Steel, David Duchovny,
Davy Crockett, Demi Lovato, Dorothy Parker, Dustin
Hoffman, Earvin Magic Johnson, Edward Norton, Emily
Bronte, Enid Blyton, Erwin Schrodinger, Estelle Getty, Esther
Williams, Ethel Barrymore, Fidel Castro, Gary Larson, Gene
Kelly, Gene Roddenberry, George Bernard Shaw, Gillian
Anderson, Guy de Maupassant, Halle Berry, Helen Mirren,
Henry Ford, Herman Melville, Hilary Swank, Hugo Chavez,
Hulk Hogan, Isaac Hayes, J.K. Rowling, Jacqueline Kennedy
Onassis, James Cameron, James Dean, Jean Piaget,
Jennifer Lawrence, Jennifer Lopez, Jim Davis, Joe Jonas,
John Stamos, Jonathon Frakes, Julia Child, Kate Beckinsale,
Kenny Rogers, Kevin Spacey, Kevin Spacey, Leon Uris, Lisa
Kudrow, Loni Anderson, LoriLoughlin, Louis Leakey, Lucille
Ball, Lynda Carter, M. Night Shyamalan, Madonna, Mae
West, Marcel Duchamp, Martha Stewart, Martin Sheen, Mata
Hari, Matt Leblanc, Matthew Perry, Maxfield Parrish, Melanie
Griffith, Meriwether Lewis (of Lewis and Clark, explorers),
Michael Beihn, Mick Jagger, Mila Kunis, Napoleon
Bonaparte, Neil Armstrong, Norman Schwarzkopf Jr., Ogden
Nash, Orville Wright, Patrick Swayze, Percy Bysshe Shelley,
Pete Sampras, Peter Jennings, Peter O'Toole, Ray Bradbury,

Reverend Jerry Falwell, Robert De Niro, Robert Redford, Roger Federer, Roman Polanski, Ron Paul, Rosalynn Carter, Sam Elliot, Sandra Bullock, Sean Penn, Sharon Creech, Shelley Winters, Simon Bolivar, Stanley Kubrick, Suzanne Collins, Taylor Momsen, Tipper Gore, Tom Brady, Tony Bennett, Usain Bolt, Veronica Roth, Vivica A. Fox, Wes Craven, Wesley Snipes, Whitney Houston, William Clark (of Lewis and Clark, explorers), Wilt Chamberlain, Woody Harrelson, Yves Saint Laurent, Zelda Fitzgerald

Appendix 3: Moon Signs, Ascendants (Rising Signs) and Planets

The natal zodiac is like a snapshot of the sky at the moment of birth. Planetary positions are believed to influence various aspects of personality and fortune.

The sun, moon, and ascendant (rising sign) are the primary astrological forces, though planets also play a role. Most people know their sun signs, but few know their ascendants or their other planetary signs.

The sun sign provides information about basic character and a framework for the rest of the natal zodiac. However, other elements such as the rising sign (also known as the ascendant) and moon sign affect the way the sun sign is expressed.

The Rising Sign (Ascendant)

The rising sign determines the outward expression of personality, or the way in which a person interacts with the external world. It can be described as the public persona or mask. It also indicates how an individual is likely to be perceived by others (how he or she comes across socially).

When the sun and ascendant are in the same or similar signs, a person behaves in a way that is consistent with his or her inner character. When the rising sign is very different from the sun sign, the individual is likely to be pulled in competing directions or to send out signals that don't match inner feelings, which increases the likelihood of being misunderstood by others. While such conflicts can make life difficult, they are also a source of creativity and a spur to achievement.

The Moon

The moon sign is the private persona, only likely to be seen in adulthood by those very close to the person. The moon rules over childhood, and people are more likely to express their moon sign personalities when they are young. In adulthood, the moon's influence is usually hidden, relegated to the secret emotional life, though an individual may openly express the moon sign persona in times of stress or other emotional extremes.

The moon also represents the mother and other female forces in a person's life. The placement of the moon in a natal chart can indicate the types of relationships and interactions a person is likely to have with women.

Other Planets

Other planets also play a role in shaping the qualities that make up an individual. Each of the planets has a particular sphere of influence, and its effects will be determined by the sign in which the planet falls and the aspects it makes to other planets:

Mercury: all forms of mental activity and communication including speaking and writing, the intellect, intelligence, reason, perception, memory, understanding, assimilation of information, and critical thinking

Venus: love, affection, pleasure, beauty, sex appeal, art, romantic affairs, adornment, social graces, harmony, and friendship

Mars: physical energy, will power, temper, assertiveness, boldness, competitiveness, impulsiveness, forcefulness, aggression, action, accidents, destructiveness, courage, and sex drive

Jupiter: luck and fortune, optimism, generosity, expansiveness, success, higher education, law, medicine, philosophy, abundance, and spirituality

Saturn: hard work, responsibility, character, strength of will, endurance, hard karma, difficulties, obstacles, hardship, the ability to see a task through to completion, authority, diligence, limitations, self-control, stability, patience, maturity, restriction, and realism

Uranus: progressiveness, change, originality, invention, innovation, technology, science, rebellion, revolution, sudden events and opportunities, awakenings, shocks, flashes of genius, eccentricity, unconventionality, unusual circumstances or events, independence, visionary ideas, and occult interests

Neptune: imagination, intuition, mysticism, dreams, fantasies, compassion, psychic abilities, visions, spirituality, strange events, the subconscious, repressed memories, glamour, mystery, insanity, drama, addiction, ideals, inspiration, transcendence, artistic sensibilities, and creative genius

Pluto: power, transformation, release of dormant forces, change, the depths of the subconscious, suppressed energies, death, rebirth, regeneration, sex, jealousy, passion, obsession, intensity, creation and destruction, beginnings and endings that occur simultaneously (one thing ending so that another can begin), secrets, mystery, undercurrents, precognition, personal magnetism, and extremes of personality

How to Find Your Moon, Ascendant, Planetary Placements, and Aspects

Astrodienst (www.Astro.com) offers free chart calculation, so you can use this site to find your planetary placements and aspects and your rising sign (for the rising sign, you will need your time of birth as well as the date and place).

References

Bugler, C. (Ed.). (1992). *The Complete Handbook of Astrology*. Marshall Cavendish Ltd., Montreal, 1992.

Cafe Astrology. CafeAstrology.com.

Castille, D. (2000). *Sunny Day for a Wedding*. Les Cahiers du RAMS.

Sachs, G. (1998). *The Astrology File: Scientific Proof of the Link Between Star Signs and Human Behavior*. Orion Books Ltd., London.

Woolfolk, J.M. (2001). *The Only Astrology Book You'll Ever Need*. Madison Books, Lanham, MD.

Printed in Great Britain
by Amazon